MW00830827

Hypnosis for Happiness

Creative Journey Publishing, Sammamish 2023

Creative Journey Publishing, Sammamish 2023
Published in the United States of America

Author: Anna Margolina
Edited by Beata Jachulski Baker
Formatting by Polgarus Studio

Copyright 2023 Anna Margolina (narrative)
ISBN: 979-8-9881567-1-0

Creative Journey Publishing, Sammamish 2023

Hypnosis for Happiness

Feel Good and Live Your Dreams

Dr. Anna Margolina, Ph.D.

Creative Journey Publishing, Sammamish 2023

Contents

Foreword

"Hypnosis For Happiness: Feel Good and Live your Dreams"
is a precious gem for people of all ages. After reading it, you'll
not just feel GOOD; you'll feel TERRIFIC! That's because
Dr. Anna's friendly wisdom and adorable sense of humor
easily brings forth the precious gifts inside of you.

As you do what Dr Anna tells you to do her practical step-
by step approach makes even complex science easy to
understand and use. She seems to know just how to speak to
you where you really live as you fall in love with who you are
and who you are becoming.

So, in-joy and out-joy yourself; then celebrate the perfect you
physically, mentally, spiritually and emotionally ... you deserve
it!

Shelley Stockwell-Nicholas, PhD
President of the International Hypnosis Federation

Your Happiness Now

"Imagination is more important than knowledge.
Knowledge is limited; imagination encircles the world."

Albert Einstein

Are you living your dream life? Are you living YOUR dream life, and not a life somebody else dreamed for you? Do you want to live a life which you have dreamed for yourself, and make it happen exactly as you have dreamed it?

Many hypnotherapy clients come to me with different problems yet the same desire – to feel good. Often, hypnotherapy is their last hope, because they have tried everything else. As they look at me with their eyes misted with tears, they tell a tale of a never-ending battle for feeling better about themselves; doing better in their life and relationships; and becoming a better parent, partner, human being, or citizen. And I always say, "Congratulations! You've made the decision to be happy, and do better. This is the most important step. The rest are technical details."

My first question for you is: "Do you want to be happy and feel good?" Pause for a moment, and write down all the reasons why you want to be happy and feel good. Then write down all the reasons why you believe the reasons you just wrote are valid and important for you. Finally, list all the reasons you deserve to be happy and feel good.

Next, take a deep breath, close your eyes, and allow yourself to daydream for a few minutes. What will it be like to live a life you truly enjoy? What will be different when you feel good? What will change because you feel better about yourself?

Did you enjoy your dream? Was it easy to imagine yourself already achieving your heart's desire? Congratulate yourself – you have already started hypnotizing yourself to be happy and feel good.

After deciding you absolutely want and desire to live your life as you want to live it, the next step is to decide to be happy **now**. Not when that perfect new lover waltzes into your life (or that boring old lover waltzes out of it). Not when you finally get your dream job, more money, more friends, a promotion, a better year, more good luck, or achieve world peace. **NOW!**

Do it now! The future never arrives.

Happiness is not a goal. Achieving a goal releases a temporary rush of dopamine and true happiness results in an exquisite mix of chemicals very similar to those you generate when you are in love. True and lasting happiness doesn't come from reaching a goal. It comes from falling in love with your life, and making the decision to stay there.

One big obstacle to being happy is (paradoxically) an aversion to any negativity. If you wear a phony mask of joy when you feel bad inside, you feel disconnected and incongruent. When you honor all emotions and celebrate joy, you have a better relationship with your body your mind and others.

Today, falling in love with your life and being happy is easier than ever. We have neuroscience, hypnosis, neuro-linguistic programming, ancient spiritual practices, and experts who are highly skilled in using all these tools. My favorite tool is hypnosis, because it is easy to learn and self-administer, it works fast, and it has no side-effects. Hypnosis helps you to master your mind *and* become the mastermind of your life. You stop fighting with your negative thoughts and tendencies (or expecting other people to change to make you happier). Instead, you teach your mind to open to a full range of your emotional experiences, feel more alive, and think with more clarity — all while bringing increasing happiness into your daily life.

This book honors your journey to happiness. Follow the activities in this book, and you will learn to hypnotize yourself to experience more and more happiness every day.

I suggest dedicating a special time for your happiness hypnosis every day. Generally, morning or the time right before sleep are the best times to make lasting and positive changes. Reserve 20 to 30 minutes every morning, and 10 to 15 minutes before sleep to do your intentional and focused practice. Think of it as learning a new language, or learning to play a musical instrument. Celebrate every accomplishment, and give yourself plenty of encouragement. Each activity is designed to give you a boost of happiness immediately, while building your ability to experience more happiness and to have more fun.

If you have questions, want to share your experiences, or desire to go deeper into your happiness journey, reach out to me at Anna@AMargolina.com.

I am delighted to hear from you!

Lovingly yours,
Dr. Anna

CHAPTER 1

How to Have More Energy (and Much More Time)

"So we find that the three possible solutions of the great problem of increasing human energy are answered by the three words: food, peace, work."

Nikola Tesla

Energy is the true currency of your happy life. When you feel energized and uplifted, it is easier to make good decisions, take inspired actions, and feel terrific. Did you know that your energy is quite real, and not just something people with

7

crystals and Tarot cards are talking about? Yes! In your physical body, you have the same electromagnetic energy which powers up your phone, or comes to your house when you flip on the light switch. Every cell in your body is powered up by electricity. When you have enough energy, you shine from inside out, and your body has enough fuel to serve your needs. When you are depleted, even the simplest task (such as getting out of bed in the morning) can be impossible. Let's begin to explore your energy.

DO THIS:

Take a deep breath, and relax your palms. Place your palms facing each other in front of you as if you were holding a medium sized ball. Focus on the space between your open palms, and imagine a glowing ball of light between your palms. Slowly begin to move your palms towards each other, and stop just short of them touching each other. Then slowly start moving them away from each other. Do it a few times, and focus on noticing any sensations in your palms and fingers.

Some people feel the energy right away. Others need a bit more time to focus in order to start feeling the subtle sensations. They can be experienced as tingling, warmth, pressure, buzzing, or movement. Some people can see a faint glow between their palms. This is what ancient Tao masters in China were calling Qi or Chi – life force. Today, modern science recognizes it as the subtle flow of bio-electromagnetic energy through all living bodies.

Did you know that your own cells make this energy? As you breathe air and eat food, your body performs an alchemical process which turns these material substances – air and food – into living light in your body.

Your body uses this light for everything. It produces new proteins, makes new cells, repairs damaged cells, and destroys old and sick cells. It uses this light for digestion, breathing, the heartbeat, physical movement, emotions, ideas, and words. Anywhere in your body where there is movement and light, there is life force energy, or Qi, powering it up.

Therefore, the first condition of being happy is having enough Qi to do the things that make you happy (and feel happy) when you do them.

Your energy is the true treasure of your life.

Energy is like the money you pay to have your experiences and be alive. When you have enough energy, you can quickly do what needs to be done, and you can have fun doing it. When you are in energy debt, you don't feel good. And you have to repay the debt over a long time, even when you have stopped depleting yourself.

Most people deplete themselves because they want to be more productive. They achieve professional expanse at the expense of personal rest and replenishment. But when your biological batteries are empty, every task takes longer and longer, and you are continually stressed and fatigued. Time and energy are closely related. By learning how to replenish and regenerate your energy reserves, and by ensuring that your bio-batteries are fully charged, you can have more energy; have more time to be happy and productive; and have experiences you enjoy.

Let's learn some simple ways to make sure you have enough energy.

DO THIS:

1. **Take a deep breath, hold it for a moment, and slowly let it out. Take another deep breath to the full capacity of your lungs, hold it for a moment, and slowly let it out. Now wiggle your toes, smile into your toes, and take a deep breath. Imagine the breath going all the way from your toes up to your crown. Follow the breath with your eyes. Hold your breath, and smile**

into your crown. Exhale with the nice, relaxed sound of "aah!"

2. Stand up, and slowly lift your arms up as you inhale. Pause at the top of your breath, and slowly lower your arms as you exhale. Shake your arms. Repeat a few times.

3. Open your arms wide, as if giving the world a big hug as you inhale. Smile into the universe. Pause. Wrap your arms around yourself, and give yourself a hug as you exhale. Smile into your heart.

4. Notice how it feels to give yourself the gift of a full breath.

Digestion and Circulation

Your digestive system needs good circulation to ensure that all the food you eat is used well, and sent on its way to your cellular power stations. Simple ways to activate your digestion and circulation include abdominal breathing, laughter, and belly rubs.

DO THIS:

1. Touch your navel with both hands, and slowly inhale while gently inwardly contracting your abdomen. Pay attention to your body's sensations. There should be no discomfort. Follow your body's cues. Your hands are there just to ensure that you are moving your abdomen in. With practice, you will be able to move your abdomen more. In the beginning, move it as far as your comfort allows.

2. Pause, and continue to press lightly. Then slowly exhale, expanding your abdomen outward. Repeat a few times.

3. Place your palms on your abdomen, and imagine your belly as a bouncing ball of joy. Discharge a big belly laugh, feeling your belly dancing under your palms. Vocalize joyfully: Ho-ho-ho! Ha-ha-ha! Hee-hee-hee!

4. Finally, gently rub your abdomen with a circular motion, and smile into it, thinking loving and caring thoughts. Imagine that your brain and your eyes are shining rays of healing energy directly into your digestive system.

You just activated your digestive system.

Move with Intention to Move Energy

Ancient Tao masters in China developed a system of moving Qi through the body, and recharging bio-batteries, which they called Qigong (Qi=life force, Gong=work). Modern science now confirms that moving slowly while being relaxed and focused on your body helps to transfer your subtle energy, and recharge your bio-batteries. There is nothing mysterious about it. Your energy moves with the flow of your inner fluids (blood, lymph, spinal fluid), with the flow of chemical messengers in your tissues, and with the flow of electrical impulses through your nerves. By focusing your mind, relaxing your body, and moving with intention, you can become a Qigong master of your own mind.

You can do Qigong while walking, vacuuming floors, doing dishes, playing with your kids, or gardening. You can incorporate Qigong into any activity. The key is to s-l-o-w down, focus your mind, and visualize moving your energy as you move your body.

DO THESE:

- Stand with your feet shoulder-width apart. Imagine your feet as having roots connecting you to the ground. Slowly lift your relaxed arms up, palms down, as you inhale. Then slowly lower your relaxed arms as you exhale. Next, imagine strings of light connecting your palms and fingers to the ground. As you inhale and very slowly lift your arms, imagine pulling these strings of light up from out of the ground. As you lower your arms, imagine absorbing the light into your palms.

- Using the same stance, lift your arms (palms up) as if asking for a blessing. Imagine your fingers becoming very long, and reaching all the way up into the universe. Breathe light through your fingers, and imagine power flowing back to you. Next, slowly bring your palms to your navel, and imagine Qi flowing into your abdomen.

- Slowly shake your entire body. Shake your arms, shake your bottom, shake your chest, shake your belly. Then stand still, and turn your attention inward. Listen to your body, look into your body, feel into your body, and smile into your body.

When done daily, these simple exercises will help you rebuild your energy, and ensure that you have sufficient reserves. They also will help you become more aware of your energy, and become better at focusing and directing it.

Hypnosis for More Energy

Hypnosis is a way of talking to yourself with clear intention and purpose. Closing your eyes helps you focus on every suggestion. Deep breathing adds life to every suggestion. Relaxation helps your body absorb beneficial suggestions like a sponge. You talk to your brain and your body. You learn to direct your own thinking. You learn to be in control of your decisions and your thoughts.

Take a few deep full breaths and close your eyes. Memorize the following suggestions (feel free to adjust them to your liking), and say them to yourself inside your mind. Or record them, and listen with your eyes closed.

"I am mindful of my energy. I am responsible for my energy, and how I use it. I breathe fully. I love breathing fully. I am mindful of my breathing. My breath is my gift. I am mindful of what I put in my body. I make good food choices. I eat to replenish my energy. I am mindful of my body. I move my body with intention. I love mindful movements. I rest my body when I need to recharge. I replenish my batteries. Every day, I am becoming more energetic and alive."

A Thought to Consider
Good Recipe and Bad Recipe

Have you ever struggled with a new or unfamiliar task? What happened? Did you get frustrated? Did you want to give up? Or did you decide to roll up your sleeves, and figure it out?

Think of a time when you decided to figure something out, and you acted on that decision. You took steps to figure it out. Perhaps it seemed hopeless at first, but maybe you were very determined. You invested hundreds of hours, you experimented, tweaked it, read a book, watched a video, and consulted an expert. And it finally clicked.

Suddenly, what was initially an effortful, tedious, and frustrating struggle became easier and easier, until you realized you were enjoying it. What happened?

To help understand this process, let's take a look at cooking. In order to successfully prepare a delicious meal, you need to take a few moving pieces into account.

You need food items such as carrots, onions, and potatoes; you need kitchen appliances and utensils; you need a source of heat, and you need a source of water.

And most of all, you need you, the cook – with your physical body.

And your physical body needs your mind; seemingly immaterial, but quite real.

Finally, you need a good recipe. If you have a good recipe, you will most likely cook a good meal. If you don't have a good recipe, you might have to order take-out.

A good recipe is the practical knowledge that takes all the moving pieces into account, as well as the real physical laws governing them.

Good recipe

For example, you can put a raw egg in the eggshell into a microwave. Is it possible? Yes! And yes, you might have a pressing need to cook the egg quickly, or you might simply believe microwaving a raw egg is a good idea. But if you attempt to cook an egg in the eggshell in a microwave it will explode. You will spend a lot of time cleaning up. It is not a good recipe.

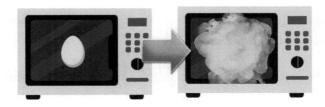

Bad recipe!

Let's look at other examples. If you keep tasting brandy while baking a cake, you might get "baked" before the cake does. If you rub your eyes after working with fresh jalapeno peppers, you might discover the importance of washing your hands after handling spicy ingredients. Recipes are not restrictions; they are practical wisdom that can save you time, and spare your nerves. It is the same with your mind. You have to make sure you use a good, time-tested recipe for changing your mind. Otherwise, you might end up burning yourself, or having a bad taste in your mouth.

A bad recipe is a recipe containing faulty instructions. There are many different variables that could account for this.

It might have worked for the author of the recipe quite by accident — a success fluke.

There might be missing steps which the original creator of the recipe didn't notice, or didn't consider important.

The recipe might require specific skills which needed to be mastered, but were never mentioned within the recipe.

The creator of this recipe might have had a very peculiar sense of taste which was drastically different from your taste.

Any recipe is a set of beliefs on how things have to be done in order to get the desired outcome.

Following a recipe is an act of trust in:

Other people's experiences and expertise;

Your own experiences and expertise;

Your own experiences, and someone else's expertise.

A good recipe is not a religion. You can change it, and make it better.

CHAPTER 2

How to Be More Playful, and Have Much More Fun

"Work consists of whatever a body is obliged to do. Play consists of whatever a body is not obliged to do."

Mark Twain

Are you playful? Or do you tend to be too serious? There is a reason why this book on being happy has a chapter on playfulness. It's now been proven that playfulness can help people deal with serious problems more creatively; lower anxiety and stress; improve relationships; make people look younger and more radiant; increase resilience to viruses and other pathogens; improve digestion; and even help in achieving a satisfying love life. There is a reason why playfulness is such a powerful factor in our overall wellbeing. When people are playful, their internal pharmacy makes potent chemicals which have positive effects on almost every aspect of our life.

DO THIS:

Think of a time when you felt happy. How did happiness feel in your body? Imagine being fully immersed in that happy memory. See what you saw, hear what you heard, and feel what you felt. Taste and smell your happy memory. Even though every person experiences happiness differently, the common denominator is the feeling of being alive.

My clients often describe it as a feeling of expansion, warmth, light, buzzing, and tingling. Everything seems brighter and more colorful. Science has identified these sensations as the effects of very special molecules produced in our body when we are happy. They are called endorphins, and are related to opiates. There are opiate receptors in our cells which bind both endorphins and exogenous (derived from the outside) opiates, such as morphine. Dr. Candace Pert, who discovered these receptors, wrote of them in her book *Molecules of Emotion*. Scientists initially planned on using endorphins to help people overcome their addiction to opiates. But these plans failed because our own endorphins turned out to be just as addictive as the opiates found in drugs.

The great thing about endorphins is that they not only make us feel happy and cause pleasant sensations in our body, but they also have many positive health effects. They improve our resistance to illnesses, reduce pain, aid in learning, and boost memory. One of the most natural ways to help your body produce more endorphins is by playing more often, and allowing more fun into your life. It's the simple truth: If you want to be happy, start doing activities which help your body make more endorphins. Simple, right? But simple only on paper. In reality, you cannot force yourself to play and have fun. Your body might be going through the motions, but if your heart isn't in it, you won't feel joyful — and your body won't make endorphins. This chapter will teach you how to become more playful.

DO THIS:

1. Take a deep breath, and close your eyes. Relax with every easy breath. Allow your mind to take you on an imaginary journey.

2. Imagine floating up from your chair, and drifting like a balloon all the way into your past. Make sure you float high enough to safely drift above all your emotional experiences while remaining quite calm and relaxed.

3. Drift all the way to your early years, and ask your unconscious mind: "Please, show me my happiest memories." Don't force your memory, and don't resist it. Just want it to happen, and allow it to happen.

4. Once you hover above a memory where you are happily doing something quite enjoyable, allow yourself to slowly drift down, and step into your memory. See what you see, hear what you hear, and feel what you feel. If there is a smell or taste, then by all means enjoy that too. Tell yourself: "I will enjoy this experience fully until my body remembers it."

5. Repeat this process with at least three other memories. Saturate your body – every nerve, every fiber of your being – with these delightful emotions of you being playful.

6. Now imagine floating all the way into your future, and infusing your future with these feelings. What do you imagine yourself doing to recall this playful and fun

feeling? What are you already doing to create this feeling? What do you want to do more of? Imagine yourself doing those things.

7. **Return to the present moment with feelings of playfulness and fun.**

The more you repeat this imaginary journey, the more your body will remember how to be playful. Playfulness will become your second nature.

Write Yourself an Actual Permission Slip to Have Fun and Play

Seriously — sit down and write yourself a free pass for fun. You will be amazed how much easier it will be to allow yourself to have more genuine and delightful fun.

Lighten Up!

Remove any pressure to have fun. Fun doesn't have to be perfect. If something isn't fun, you don't have to do it. Once you allow yourself to admit that some activities are not that enjoyable (even though other people might find them amusing) it will be easier for you to have effortless and genuine fun. Learning what makes something fun for you, and what games you truly love to play, will make being playful much easier.

Hypnosis for Playfulness

"I am naturally playful. I know how to lighten up. I give myself permission to be silly and goofy. I take being playful seriously. I create the room to be playful. I surround myself with playful and light-hearted people. I nurture my inner child. I let my inner child out to play."

A Thought to Consider
Thinking and Remembering

Think about thinking. So every thought floating to the surface of your mind may be considered true, and might trigger emotional reactions. If you are constantly bothered, tormented, and interrupted by their own thoughts, you can change it.

To take charge of your own thinking, separate your thoughts into two distinct categories: thinking, and remembering. Not only are they different in origin, but they are also neurologically different processes.

Thinking establishes new neural pathways; it also builds new connections between existing pathways.

Remembering is a process during which the same neural pathways are activated by the same internal or external event.

Thinking is a slower process which involves trial and error, contemplation, moving pieces inside one's mind, and considering different perspectives. It resembles going on a walking adventure, with the intention to explore and investigate.

Remembering is a much faster process in which you arrive at a conclusion, emotion, or a choice of action quite quickly. It resembles traveling by train. It is fast and efficient — and you have no control once you board the train.

Thinking   Remembering

One of the important roles of families and schools is helping a child integrate into society, which has a certain set of laws, rules, and beliefs. Family traditions, social conditioning, and most public education systems encourage the process of remembering and repeating, and discourage (or even severely punish) independent thinking and creating. But in biological terms, a human mind needs both processes to be well developed and thoroughly mastered in order to be effective and flexible.

Remembering creates a set of roads or structures inside the mind. It is faster to travel if you have good roads and railways. Remembered knowledge organizes the mind, and makes it efficient and quick. A musician spends a lot of time practicing music so that they can play even the most complex music pieces without any obvious effort. It takes time to learn how to read, write, or to ride a bicycle. With practice, those things become easy. But the structures of remembering can be too rigid, preventing the mind from being able to think differently. The mind becomes a train that cannot leave its tracks. Creative thinking is a skill which allows for considering different perspectives, and exploring various options. But creative thinking without good structure can lead to aimless wandering, wasting both time and energy. Now let's introduce another essential function of the brain: learning.

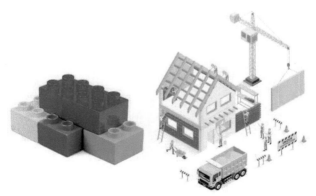

Learning

Learning is using a function of the brain called neuroplasticity to demolish, alter, or replace old structures, roads, and railways with new structures which work better, and achieve better results. In order for learning to create a new and stable structure, it has to include the process of practicing. This is a process of running the same sequence of thoughts and actions multiple times until they become instinctive, and can be trusted to the unconscious automatic functions of the mind.

CHAPTER 3

How to Be More Creative

"Creativity is intelligence having fun."

Albert Einstein.

The above quote by Albert Einstein can also be written as a formula: $C = I + F$. It might be less famous than $E = mc^2$, but to those who want to be happy, it is just as brilliant.

Creativity is the joy of finding a new and unexpected solution to an old problem. Creativity is the cry of "Eureka!" as you jump out of your bath, and dance with glee when you solve another puzzle. Creativity is combining musical notes, colors and shapes, words and phrases, and fabrics and patterns, until your whole being vibrates with delight at what you created. Creativity helps in business, learning, relationships, sports and (yes) in art. It is good for your health, and it is good for your life. When you know how creativity works, you can help yourself become more creative. This will add more vibrancy and happiness to your life.

When I start working with a new hypnotherapy client, I explain to them that the process is just like when they were children, and could pretend that a cardboard box was a medieval castle. They could live inside their stories so fully they became real. Children have a much closer relationship with magic than most adults. But inside every adult there is a child full of wonder and magic and light. When we tap into this childhood wonder, we start living our magic. This is the secret to creativity.

There are three rules of creativity:

1. **It needs space.**
2. **It thrives in the dream mind.**
3. **It cannot be forced, commanded, or ordered.**

Let's explore some ways to become more creative. Remember: You already were a creative genius when you were a child. It is only a matter of reminding (re-minding) yourself how to do it with ease.

Schedule Some Dedicated Time to Do Absolutely Nothing

Resist the urge to fill 100% of your time with busyness. Get comfortable with being idle. It can be 10 minutes, 30 minutes, or an hour. It can be a whole day of doing nothing. You decide.

Allow your thoughts to emerge, but do not expect yourself to produce something of genius every time you do it.

At first, doing nothing might be the most difficult job you ever had. Eventually you might notice a tingle of curiosity.

Like a shy child, your mind will begin to reach out beyond its everyday routine. Observe how your mind starts touching the world around you.

If you get a twinkle of desire to play with crayons or paper or rocks or leaves, do so. Imagine there is a gentle current of curiosity flowing through you. Follow the current.

Think Of Two Different Things, and Find How They Might Be Alike

"Why is a raven like a writing desk?" (From *Alice in Wonderland* by Lewis Carroll.)

In NLP (Neuro-Linguistic Programming, which is a form of hypnosis), the above exercise is called "The Fuzzy Brain Exercise." In *Alice in Wonderland*, Alice is annoyed by that riddle because it has no answer. However, the question is not that random. One way to make your brain more creative is to think of two completely unrelated things, and let your brain come up with some connection between them. It is an excellent game to play with friends (and children). Every time you play it, your brain has to find a way to connect the two concepts, building more connections. The more fun you have, the more you want to play this game.

Just Imagine

Every child is highly imaginative. Because imagination is rarely valued in a typical school setting, few adults remain highly imaginative. But that doesn't mean imagination cannot be reclaimed. Playing with your imagination is fun, and can greatly improve your happiness. One reason many adults are unhappy is because they let their imagination run wild outside of their awareness. Worry is a perfect example of the misuse of imagination. In order to worry, one has to imagine various disastrous scenarios. They become so real they start affecting one's emotions. This is a superpower misused. The good news is that the same imagination used to create a doomsday scenario for the future can be used to create wonderful dreams, bright hopes, and delicious goals.

Doodle!

Just put your pen to paper, and let it create shapes and lines. Be curious about what comes out. Doodling stimulates your creative brain, and allows new neural connections to form in your body.

Ask Your Inner Critic to Step Outside

Since creativity cannot be forced or commanded, ask your inner critic to take a backseat while you let your intelligence have some fun. Robert Dilts, an NLP expert, analyzed Walt Disney's mental process for innovations. In this strategy, you take on roles of **The Dreamer, The Realist,** and **The Critic** in this order.

First, The Dreamer comes up with a creative idea in a judgment-free space. Next, The Realist points to the part of the idea which might be unrealistic or undoable. Then, The Critic steps in, and finds flaws and issues. The Dreamer takes over again. And on the cycle goes.

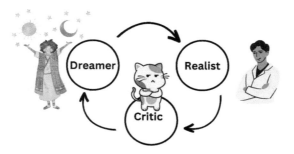

Walt Disney knew how to bring his ideas to fruition. He also knew how to make his ideas fresh and creative. Instead of letting The Realist and The Critic shut down the creative process, he learned to let The Dreamer dream freely. If your critic begins to interfere with your creativity, very politely ask them to step aside and wait until you finish playing with your mind.

Learn to Engage In the Creative Struggle; Then Relax, Let Go, and Let It Be

This part might be challenging to those who need instant solutions, or who learned to work hard and press forward until they succeeded. But because all new solutions require the brain to find new connections and new ways of thinking, this pressure might send your thought process into an old, pre-programmed, and well-trodden path. Therefore, once you hand your creative mind a question, a riddle, or a problem to solve, let it go. Go do something else. Your unconscious mind will continue working on its assigned puzzle. It is not uncommon for people to struggle trying to solve a problem, only to receive a perfect solution in their sleep.

The Russian scientist Dmitri Mendeleev saw The Periodic Table of Elements in his sleep. Another scientist, August Kekulé, went to sleep trying to find the way the molecule of benzene was arranged. As he fell asleep, he saw atoms arranging themselves into a snake biting its tail in his dreams. Upon awakening, he realized that the molecule of benzene was a ring; it had a cyclic structure.

Use the strategy of alternating hard and focused work with deep relaxation, or trance, or even sleep. This shifting of intention will allow you to come up with creative solutions more often, and experience more of the bliss of creativity.

Hypnosis for Creativity

I am creative. It is easy for me to come up with new ideas and solutions. I make room for creativity. I play with my mind often. I nurture my creative genius every day. I play with ideas. I find inspiration in nature. Creative people inspire my creativity. I enjoy works of art. I give myself permission to fail and make mistakes. I entertain my mind with new ideas daily.

A Thought to Consider
Neurons That Fire Together
Wire Together

The functional unit of the nervous system is the neuron. It is a cell with many tentacles, some of which are very long and branched. The human brain contains billions of neurons. In order for us to think, feel, or remember, neurons have to:

1. Become electrically active – as neuroscientists say, neurons "fire" an electric potential, which runs through their cell membrane until it reaches the end of the tentacle.

2. Transfer the electric potential to another neuron, which in turn will "fire."

3. "Fire" neurons in a certain sequence or pattern, which will be decoded by the mind as information such as an image, letter, word, sound, sensation, or an idea.

The basic law of neuroscience states "Neurons that fire together, wire together." Every thought is created by millions of neurons connecting in a certain pattern. When you think the same thought repeatedly, neurons form a stronger connection – they "wire" together. Every time you repeat the same thinking pattern, you fortify the connection. A sequence of thoughts that is repeated over and over becomes an automatic pattern. Some patterns are engraved into the brain very quickly. This happens when a sequence of thoughts and actions is triggered by a very strong emotion – usually fear. The next time something triggers this sequence, it runs on its own. Fear wires neurons instantly.

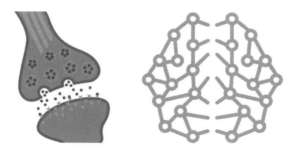

Since electricity is a form of energy, we can say that thoughts are energy flowing through your brain. Every time you think, you send energy flowing through your neurons.

Whether you think a happy thought or a depressing thought, it is all simply electricity. In this regard, we cannot judge the energy of the thought to be "bad" or "good." But thoughts do trigger emotions, and different emotions affect our physiology in very different ways. From this point of view, we can talk about the energies in our body as being either health-promoting, or toxic.

The reason our body is affected by thoughts is that it also has neural networks. As scientific studies now show, there are dense neural networks in our heart, gut, and all major organs. There is even a dense neural network in our skin. This is why a gentle, loving touch feels so good. The neural networks in our gut are so significant, scientists are now talking about "the gut brain." All these networks contain neurons, which can fire together, wire together, and create patterns of thinking and feeling.

CHAPTER 4

How to Sleep Well Every Night

Do you sleep well? Do you get enough sleep? Do you wake up refreshed and replenished, with a smile greeting the new day?

Sleep is essential. During our nighttime repose, our body is not idle. Our brain is busy clearing itself of the toxic by-products of our metabolism, inflammatory molecules, and superfluous information. Ultra-low delta brain waves activate a special cleaning service of the brain – the glymphatic system – which flushes away all the junk from our brain fluid. Our entire body uses our sleep time to repair and regenerate its structures. And our inner computer uses this time to reorganize our memories, and move them into long-term storage. Sleep is good for you, and good sleep is your best asset if you want to be healthier and happier. Pleasant and vivid dreams add joy and magic to your everyday reality. With some practice, you can learn to remember your dreams better, and even start receiving insightful messages from your inner mind. Learning how to sleep deeper, and wake up more refreshed and regenerated can add happiness to your life. You will begin to truly live your dream life.

In this chapter, you will learn simple sleep habits and healthy sleep meditations which will turn your nighttime experience into a dream journey.

Eat Light Before Sleep

Nobody likes to go to sleep feeling hungry, but having a full belly can make falling asleep more difficult. Make your last meal of the day light, and leave at least three hours (more is better) between your meal and sleep time. Digestion requires a lot of energy, and since it is a very important process, it has energy priority. Going to sleep after most of your digestion is complete allows your body to have enough energy for your brain cleanup, body regeneration, and memory organization.

Never Go to Sleep Exhausted

It may sound strange to rest before sleep, but your body actually needs energy to go to sleep — and it definitely needs energy to do its nightly maintenance tasks. Leave some time before sleep to wind down and relax. Take a warm, relaxing bath with your favorite bath oils or salts. Read a good book. Go for a walk, or spend some quiet time with your family or pets. Creating room for rest and relaxation before sleep will allow you to drift off to sleep more easily. You will sleep more soundly, and will wake up more refreshed and regenerated.

Make Your Room Dark

Humans evolved to sleep during the night, and be active during the day. When you are awake and alert, the amino acid tryptophan is converted in your body into the neurotransmitter serotonin, which makes you feel uplifted, happy, and energized. This reaction is triggered by light falling on your retinas. When it is dark, another reaction takes place. Serotonin is converted into melatonin, a special chemical which makes you very sleepy. Melatonin is a wonder molecule which helps your body regenerate, boosts your immune system, and makes your skin younger. It even has anti-cancer properties. It is good to have more melatonin in your body. Many modern humans do not make enough melatonin during the night because their room is never completely dark. Light seeps in from the outside, and LED displays from computers, cell phones, and nightlights glow throughout most bedrooms. If you want your body to feel refreshed, rested, and rejuvenated in the morning, make your room as dark as possible. You can cover the windows with blackout curtains, and turn off (or remove) all electronics for the night.

Hypnotize Yourself to Go to Sleep

Hypnosis is a natural state through which you briefly pass on your way from full wakefulness to deep slumber. When you are fully awake, your brain mostly generates high frequency, busy beta brain waves. As you relax, slower and larger alpha brain waves spread throughout your brain. Next, there is a brief period of theta brain wave activity. Finally, the brain goes into deep sleep, with very slow and large delta waves taking over. In the REM (Rapid Eye Movement) stage of sleep, the brain has a wild mix of all brain waves. This is the dream stage. Self-hypnosis allows you to enter the dream stage by intentionally switching your brain to alpha, and then theta, brain wave activity. From there, going into the delta brain wave state is very easy.

DO THIS:

Begin with the mantra, "It is my intention to enter the dream world." Repeat this three times in your head, imagining speaking in a calm, relaxed, and sleepy voice.

You can adjust your words as needed so they perfectly communicate your honest desire to go to sleep.

Next, imagine some downward process. I like the image of an elevator. Some people prefer an escalator. Some people like to walk down stairs. Whatever you choose will be perfect for you.

Now, slowly and sleepily begin counting down from 10 to 1, imagining going deeper and deeper with every number you count. If you're using an elevator image, imagine it going down from the 10th floor to the 1st floor. Then imagine continuing down to the basement. If using an escalator image, imagine going deeper and deeper to a peaceful place. If using a staircase image, imagine walking down slowly, relaxing with every step.

10 - Going deeper...relaxing...calm...peaceful...

9 - Even deeper...even more relaxing...calm...peaceful... all is well...

8 - Deeper...I am safe...I am feeling very relaxed... peaceful...

7 - Sleepy...relaxing...deeper...

6 - Sleepy...

You might never reach the 1st floor, and just drift to sleep. Or you can imagine going deeper and deeper, to 0, -1, -2...

Here is another way to hypnotize yourself to sleep:

Take a few nice, deep, easy breaths, and close your eyes. Now, state your intention to enter the dream reality. Start imagining a pleasant and relaxing place. Be there 100%. Become curious (much like *Alice in Wonderland*). Wait for something to change. Become more curious. Watch for more changes. Maybe a story will begin to unfold. Follow the White Rabbit. It might not actually be a white rabbit, but it doesn't matter. It just as surely will lead you to your own Wonderland, and you will not even notice how you drift into a peaceful and pleasant slumber.

This next method is perfect for busy thinkers and doers:

Instead of lying awake worrying about not being able to go to sleep, take a deep breath, and close your eyes. Think of some activity you will be doing tomorrow, or sometime in the near future. Make sure it is a pleasant and rewarding activity, like preparing a birthday party. Think of how you want to feel when you are doing it. What is the ideal way you want it to go? Then begin building this reality in your mind. If it is a birthday party, imagine arranging flowers and plates on the table, decorating the room, and welcoming guests in bright, festive clothes. Smile at your beautiful work. The deeper you engage with your imagination, the more you step into the dream world. Suddenly, you are dreaming for real.

Keep a Dream Journal

Dreams are fleeting. How often have you woken up thinking, "What an amazing dream!" Then it would be gone, and you couldn't remember it. You can help yourself remember your dreams— and even receive some wise messages from your deep mind — if you begin keeping a dream journal.

Put a notebook and a pen next to your bed. The moment you wake up, if you still remember your dream, write it down. Then ask yourself, "What does my mind want to tell me?" The unconscious mind thinks in metaphors. Just as in children's fairy tales where animals have human emotions, and represent human problems, so it is in the dream mind. It is always talking to you — and it makes sense to listen.

Pay attention to emotions and attitudes. Let's imagine you had a dream about a cat who was happy, and then upset, and then happy again. Imagine being this cat. Observe the dream from the cat's perspective. What do you notice? Where in your life do you feel this feeling? Now, let's imagine that in the same dream there is a person who pets the cat, and then becomes angry with the cat, and then pets it again. Be that person. Experience the story from this person's perspective. Where in your life do you experience similar feelings? After you've imagined being every character, ask yourself, "What is the message?" Write it down.

What I noticed for myself and my clients is that the more I listen to my dream mind, the more it communicates to me. My dreams became a big and happy part of my everyday life. I live in my waking state, and then I travel and have adventures in my dreams. Then I wake up, and receive great insights and wisdom.

Release All Negative Emotions Before Sleep

Negative emotions are not bad. It is natural and healthy to have them. But if they have not been properly processed or expressed during the day, they should not be kept trapped in the body.

DO THIS:

- Sit up straight in a chair. Shake your arms a few times, and then put your hands on your lap.

- Move your spine from side to side to relieve the tension. Stretch. Yawn. Move your shoulders.

- Next, notice any unpleasant tension in your body. Focus on that area. Smile into this area. Imagine gathering whatever energy you are holding there. Inhale, and then exhale with a long "aah" breath. Imagine letting go. Imagine all that tension going down into the ground.

- Rest. Smile into your body. Imagine shining your light into it. Notice if you're holding any unpleasant tension anywhere else. Repeat the process.

- When you've released all your tension, lift your arms up, stretch, and look up. Imagine reaching out to the universe. Inhale, and pull a ball of calming relaxing energy from above through your head, shoulders, and torso, all the way to your toes. Exhale all the way down.

You will immediately feel lighter and sleepier. You might start yawning, and your eyes might tear up.

Do this release process every night before you go to sleep. You will notice that you sleep deeper, and wake up happier and much more rested.

A Thought to Consider
Thinking Is Chemistry

When two people fall in love immediately and passionately, we say they have "chemistry" between them. If you have ever been in the same room with two people who are madly and passionately in love, you know this mysterious "chemistry" can be almost palpable. We know now that falling in love alters our body chemically. What most people do not realize is that every emotional state has chemistry. Just as love makes people look more radiant, and feels really good in the body, every feeling has measurable physiological effects on the body.

Dr. Candace Pert discovered that besides neurons, other cells in our body have receptors for the molecules of emotions, which are mostly peptides. When a cellular receptor recognizes a certain peptide, they resonate and vibrate together, triggering a cascade of biochemical changes. Such changes might tell the cell to produce certain proteins or perform other physiological tasks. Emotions can boost or diminish immunity, elevate or lower blood pressure, relax muscles or create more muscle tension, etc. They can activate or silence various genes. Emotions and their molecules are now considered a bridge between our immaterial mind and our physical body.

This means that every time we think, we are writing ourselves a prescription which orders your neurology to dispense a unique mixture of chemical compounds. This means that we can look at thinking as the "cooking" of a certain chemistry in our body. Some recipes boost our strength and immune system, make us look younger and more beautiful, and help us think more clearly and solve problems faster. Other recipes might rob us of our strengths, paralyze our will, deplete our energy, cause our body to have pains and aches, increase inflammation, and fog our thinking and reasoning. Therefore, learning how to use your own brain and body to make yourself happier will not only make your life better, but can actually improve your health and wellbeing.

CHAPTER 5

How to Love Eating Healthy

Many years ago, I was on a plane. The elderly gentleman next to me greeted me politely, and then asked, "Have you read Sherlock Holmes?"

I loved Sherlock Holmes when I was a kid, so I nodded enthusiastically.

He said, "I recently went to London, and I expected to see that gray, gloomy, foggy city described by Sir Conan Doyle, but it was quite clear and bright. Do you know why?"

I didn't know.

"Coal."

"What?"

"Coal. They stopped using coal-burning stoves. In the past, every house had a chimney, and the whole city was gray and gloomy because of all the smog."

I remembered this conversation when I started learning how to eat healthy without making it a daily struggle.

There are 37.2 trillion cells in your body, and they all have their "stoves." Only instead of coal, they use food. Practically your entire body is designed for the very purpose of making sure you have enough energy. You have your lungs because you need oxygen to make energy from food. You have your intricate digestive system because you need to turn your food into very tiny particles that can be used by your cells. You have your heart and a system of blood vessels to deliver oxygen and fuel to every cell, and take away the waste. And you have a complex system of waste removal because no fuel is 100% efficient. There is always waste.

Imagine every cell in your body as having its own chimney. If you use clean fuel, you produce less fog and toxicity. If you use dirty fuel which produces a lot of waste, your cells become like the thick toxic fog in which Sherlock Holmes and Doctor Watson wandered.

Food is more than just calories, fats, proteins, and carbohydrates. First of all: Food is medicine. For example, plants contain powerful protective compounds called antioxidants which are not produced in the human body, yet are essential for its health and wellbeing. Antioxidants protect our skin from premature aging, reduce inflammation, and neutralize many environmental and internally-produced toxins. Some of the best-known antioxidants are vitamin C, vitamin E, beta-carotene and other carotenoids, bioflavonoids, and resveratrol (found in red wine).

Plants are also the best source of dietary fiber which, like a broom, helps sweep the intestines clean, and makes the microbes in our gut happy and healthy. Women after 40 might appreciate that plants such as soy, pomegranate, dates, and others contain dietary compounds resembling estrogens. They are called phytoestrogens. They are much weaker than estrogens. And unlike synthetic estrogens used in hormone replacement therapy for menopause, phytoestrogens are very gentle, and have no side effects.

Second: In addition to its nutritional value, food has emotional value. Eating a delicious, well-prepared, and beautifully served meal makes the body happy, and the body produces its own happy medicine – endorphins. In addition to making us feel good, endorphins boost immunity, lower blood pressure, reduce pain, and improve digestion, breathing, and circulation.

Third: Food is a great bonding activity. Sharing a delicious meal with fun and positive people increases happiness, and promotes wellbeing on all levels.

Eating healthy means providing your body with clean fuel and good medicine, and feeling great. If you add effective breathing, good circulation, and great digestion, you will get a recipe for happiness and longevity.

Eating healthy doesn't have to be confusing, costly, or complicated. Here are some tips to start eating healthier — and to love doing it.

Small Steps Are Essential

Energy production is the foundational process in the body. If you are alive, that means whatever you have been doing has been working for you so far. You are alive! If you make massive changes all at once, your body might panic, and start fighting back. So write down your three goals: clean fuel, good medicine, and feeling great. Then imagine yourself eating food which achieves all these goals. If you hate spinach, do not include it, because you are not going to feel great while trying to force it down your throat. If you get good feelings from eating junk food that contain substances your body cannot process, it won't be clean fuel. Make a list of foods which fit all three categories, and think of where and how you can start including them into your meals.

Love Your Future Self

If you want to start eating healthier, it's probably because you have a certain vision of how you want to live your life, and how you want to look, feel, and act in the future. Imagine you have already made all the changes you wanted to make. Imagine your food fuel is so clean that your body is bright and radiant. Imagine thinking clearly and feeling great. Imagine feeling lighter and more vibrant. Imagine being in the shape and size you enjoy. Whatever you want to include in this future vision, do it! Then imagine visiting with your future self, and experiencing your dream life. Do you like it? Is there anything you need to change? Keep adjusting your vision until you

LOVE it! Not just like, but LOVE, DESIRE, and CRAVE! Then, as you begin including foods which are clean fuel and good medicine, and make you feel great, focus on this thought: "Every bite moves me closer and closer to my dream vision. Every time I choose to eat this food, I am moving closer and closer to my dream." Notice that it is in our nature to feel great when we know our dream is getting closer and closer.

Eat Colors

A very simple way to brighten your day (and your plate) while giving your body healthy and balanced nutrition is to ensure that your food has colors. Different colors reflect different energies and different chemical compositions. Vibrancy, unless it is artificially created, indicates that the food is fresh and filled with good medicine. Tomatoes are red, onions are white, zucchini are green, bananas are yellow – it is fun to play with colors, and be creative. Make it a habit to add something colorful and natural to your plate, and your body will be very happy.

Create a Sacred Space for Your Meals

Beautifully served and mindfully enjoyed food shouldn't just be reserved for the times you have guests over, or when you go to a restaurant. Let your eyes feast on your meal before you feast on it with your tastebuds.

DO THIS:

- Begin by deciding that you deserve to be nourished. Imagine your body as a temple to which you bring your best offerings. If spiritual metaphors are not for you, imagine your body as your best friend (which it is).

- Clear the space for your food. Remove clutter and electronics. Put a beautiful tablecloth or placemat on the table. If you want, add fresh flowers or other decorations.

- Serve your food on a beautiful plate, and sit down to enjoy it.

- Start with looking at your plate, and appreciating all the colors. Think of the future you are creating. And think of all the people who worked to bring this meal to your plate. Send them your gratitude. Send your gratitude to the plants and animals, and to the earth. Finally, send gratitude to yourself. (If you already say grace, you might add this gratitude ritual to your prayer.)

- Smell your food before eating it. Savor the aroma.

- Eat mindfully, chewing slowly and deliberately.

- As you swallow every bite, follow it with your mind, and smile as you do it.

- After your meal, sit quietly for a few minutes, and notice how your body responds. Clean, healthy, fresh, and nutritious food feels great when you eat it — and after you eat it.

- Say to yourself, "I make good, healthy choices for myself. I love myself. I decide what to put into my body. I feel good about my choices. I am in control. It's good to be in control of my choices. It's great to make healthy and positive choices for myself."

As you begin to feel lighter and more radiant, your body will begin to crave better and healthier choices. Eating healthy will become easier and easier. Eventually, it will become your new way of being. With clean fuel, you will have more energy, clarity, and focus. You will be able to do more in less time and without stress. Your skin will look younger, and your eyes will look brighter and clearer. Your body will feel very happy — and when your body is happy, you are happy as well.

A Thought to Consider
Inner Conflicts

Being a human child in today's society means being subjected to conflicting programming. This means that many adults find themselves in situations where, instead of having a clear chemical and physiological state ideal for problem-solving or dealing with a challenge, their neurology enters a state of conflict. From a neurological point of view, we are talking about two or more neural networks that are equally activated, but create a differently aimed response. They open the gates to certain chemicals, and alter the body's physiology in a certain way. As they pull in opposite directions, it messes up the body's chemistry and physiology.

For example, a person who is afraid of public speaking — yet has a desire to speak — might have two opposite internal states running at the same time. One might be stimulating (bold), and another might be inhibiting (timid). If your "timid" network is fully activated, you will stay quiet, and have no desire to speak. Many people are timid and do just fine. It is not a problem if everything is aligned. If only your "bold" network is activated, and this is your dominant response, you will have no problem saying what you want in front of any audience. But when both responses and sets of programming are positioned against each other, the brain cannot perform at the level which is required to successfully complete the task.

There's also sequential incongruity, in which the conflict occurs across time rather than at a particular moment. In sequential incongruity, the person fluctuates between two conflicting responses. A strong emotion commandeers all available power so other behaviors are inhibited. Then another strong emotion takes the lead, and inhibits all other behaviors and responses.

If you want to be happier, you need to learn how to negotiate with your conflicting wishes and wills, and get them all on board for smooth sailing toward your goals. This is where hypnotherapy can be very helpful.

CHAPTER 6

How to Set Excellent Goals, and Follow Through Easily

Have you ever had a goal — and achieved it? Have you ever had a goal — and **not** achieve it? What was the difference between the two?

Sometimes goals cannot be achieved because of external circumstances. Certainly, the COVID-19 pandemic of 2020 put many dreams and goals on hold, and ruined many well-thought-out plans. But often, rather than an external obstacle, internal thinking processes are hindering the achievement of a goal. In this chapter you will discover how easy it is to set goals, and follow through on them when you have a good mental strategy.

First, let's think of goals you have already achieved. They do not have to be big goals. Did you brush your teeth today? You have achieved the goal of taking care of your dental health. Did you make your bed, or prepare your breakfast? Did you successfully take your kids to school, or drive yourself to work? These are all goals which you have set and achieved.

Every goal must first become real in the energy space – in your imagination. But the goals you achieve become real, while those you never achieve stay in this imaginary space.

These are a few key characteristics of the imaginary reality:

1. **There is no time.**
2. **There is no distance.**
3. **There is no money.**
4. **Everything can happen at once.**

You can dream about going to Italy, imagine arriving there, and visualize having a great time — all at the same time. You do not have to buy a plane ticket, pack your bags, drive to the airport, spend a few hours on a plane, call an Uber, arrive at your hotel, and unpack your bags before you can actually enjoy Italy. Moving toward a goal will require spending time, traveling some distance, spending money, and employing a sequence of steps to get there. But if you never take the time to think or dream about going to Italy, you are unlikely to take any steps toward this goal. Dreaming is essential. And learning how to dream better is very important. It can make all the difference between fully engaging your executive and resourceful functions, and getting them on board; or allowing them to sabotage your efforts, and turn everything into an ordeal.

DO THIS:

Think of something you want. It is very important to think of something you actually WANT rather than what you DO NOT WANT. Now imagine sprinkling some magic dust over your dream, waving a magic wand, and making this dream real.

- See what you see. Hear what you hear. Feel what you feel. The more senses you can involve, the more your mind will be tricked into perceiving it as reality.

- Note: If your goal is not realistic, you will recognize that during this process of trying to make it real for you. For example, if you want to sprout a pair of wings, or grow 10 feet tall, it will never seem real. Your unconscious mind will know those dreams aren't possible.

- Don't worry about how (or if) you can achieve this dream. For now, tell yourself you are just trying this dream on.

- What it is like?

- Is it good for you, and for the people in your life?

- Is there anything that needs to be adjusted or changed to make it even better? If yes, make the adjustment.

Create Magnetic Attraction

Go back to your present reality. Your accomplished goal is now in the future. Do you feel something pulling you toward it? Is there magnetic attraction? Let's make it stronger!

DO THIS:

- Imagine a rubber band attached to you in the now at one end, and to you in the future at the other end. Notice that this imaginary rubber band needs to be mentally attached to your actual body. Feel the pull.

- See the rubber band vibrating as it stretches. Hear the buzzing of the rubber band as it becomes like a string.

- Now, imagine letting go. Let the rubber band pull you right into your future body. Zoom! You have arrived!

- What it is like?

- See it, feel it, listen to it, taste it, and smell it.

- Notice how good it feels.

- Let yourself bask in the sense of accomplishment. Let every cell in your body vibrate with happiness.

- With every breath, make this future bigger and brighter, and allow yourself to grow with it. How big can you make it? How much more vibrant, delightful, and exciting can you imagine yourself being as you live in this future?

The rubber band is just one image. You can also imagine magnets pulling you toward your goal, or any other device or force that creates an attraction.

Reverse Engineer It!

DO THIS:

- Imagine being in the future just after you've accomplished your goal. How do you know you've achieved it? What has to happen in order for you to know, "It is done!" It might be opening your newly published book, saying your wedding vows, seeing yourself in the mirror as you wish to appear, etc.

- Take one step back from this moment in time when you have already accomplished your goal. What had to happen right before you accomplished it?

- Step back once more. What had to happen before this?

- Keep stepping backward in time, noticing what had to happen before your dream became reality.

This process is called "reverse engineering." You start with the end result, and retrace the steps which led you there.

A real-life example:

One of my clients wanted to find a soulmate partner. When asked to imagine the end result, she imagined being with someone who is perfectly aligned with her, mentally, emotionally, physically and spiritually. When asked to go backward one step at a time, she was surprised to discover that there was quite a long process between meeting someone suitable, and moving forward together with him.

End goal: We are living together, and we are happy.

One step back: He asks me to move in with him, and I accept.

Another step back: We realize we are a perfect match.

Another step back: We are spending a lot of time together, and we enjoy each other, etc.

She also realized why she had not previously achieved this goal. Deep inside, she had a fear of letting the wrong person into her heart, ruining her good life. Reverse engineering her goal allowed her to see that there were many steps during which she could get to know a person better. And if needed, she could decide not to continue moving forward with the relationship.

Sometimes people do not know what steps they need to take. One method is to imagine looking (or sensing in any other way) from the future back to the present moment, and telling your all-knowing wise self to bring you insights, wisdom, and creative ideas to help reach your goal in the easiest and most enjoyable way. Then just let it go for a while and wait. You might "accidentally" bump into a friend or a mentor who can help you. A book might fall off your bookshelf and open to a useful page. Or something else might happen which will bring you greater clarity and direction.

Go Forward with a Good Feeling

Now you know what you need to do to reach your goal. You have a vision and a roadmap. From the present moment, think of the next logical step to start moving toward this goal. What would be the best emotion or inner state which would allow you to take this step? Do you need help? Do you need resources? Do you need to free up some time? What feeling would allow you to take this step with greater ease? For the woman in my example, her first step was to start going to places where she could actually meet new people. Her resourceful inner states were curiosity, fun, and hope. What do you need to move forward with a good feeling?

Got your feeling? Think of the last time you felt this way. Really step into the memory. Feel the feeling. Imagine taking your first step with this good feeling. Notice how much easier it is to move forward with a good feeling.

Make a Good Plan You Love

Now you can write your steps down, and create a timeline for them. You can keep attaching good feelings to every step. Leave some wiggle room for unforeseen circumstances. Plans that are too rigid do not pass the reality test. Imagine being adaptable and flexible. Imagine rerouting your plans in a good spirit. And imagine that achieving your goal is a done deal. The road you take might be different from what you initially mapped. There are many roads that can get you where you want to go. Some of them will be scenic rides, and some of them will be obstacle courses. But when you know your goal is a done deal, and you have already visited it in your imagination, and you know what it takes to get there, and you know how to move forward with good feelings, you will arrive at your destination. You might even get an inspiring story to tell after you have arrived.

CHAPTER 7

How to Be Confident, and Have Great Boundaries

"The trouble with having an open mind, of course, is that people will insist on coming along and trying to put things in it."

Terry Pratchett, *Diggers*

Once upon a time there were three little pigs who decided to build their own houses, and live in the forest happily ever after. You probably know this fairy tale. One little pig built a house out of straw, another built a house out of sticks, and the third pig decided to take a bit more time, and built a house out of bricks.

In the same forest there lived a big bad wolf. The wolf was bad from the little pigs' perspective, because he was a carnivore.

He came across the house built out of straw, and started huffing and puffing, trying to blow the house down. This was a bit of a show, because he could have just reached in through the straw to pull the little pig out. But his vain actions allowed the first little pig to escape through the back door, and run as fast as he could to his little brother's house built out of sticks. The big bad wolf — now rather enjoying this game — moved on to the stick house, and proceeded to huff and puff in an attempt to blow *that* house down. The two little pigs were smart enough to then run as fast as they could to the brick house. Once inside, they bolted the doors, and closed all the windows. Now the wolf was a bit irritated. He was getting really hungry, and all the pigs were now out of reach.

Still, he huffed and he puffed, and he pounded on the windows, and he kicked at the door, but the brick house was very well built. Eventually, the wolf met his demise by falling into a pot of boiling water while trying to get into the house through the chimney.

This story illustrates the importance of good boundaries.

Your own skin protects your body from bacteria, dirt, and other harmful intruders. Your own house protects you from people who might not have your best interests at heart. Similarly, your own mind — when it has strong boundaries — protects you from harmful and draining influences from other people.

Many people want to be more confident. However, expecting yourself to be confident without having good boundaries is like expecting your money to stay in your account while giving your password and pin number freely to anyone who asks.

The problem with mental boundaries is that — unlike the walls of your house or the barrier of your skin — they are invisible to the eye. It is not easy to notice when they are weak or damaged.

In this chapter you will learn a rarely talked about secret of great confidence and inner peace: good boundaries.

Let's start by imagining your mind is the house in which you live. And like a hermit crab or a turtle, you carry this house with you wherever you go.

Everything that comes in contact with your mind has the potential to influence you. This means it can harm you, deplete you, or even kill you. Great confidence and peace of mind are graced with the knowledge that whatever might be going on outside of you will not be able to penetrate the boundaries of your mind. You can choose whom to invite into your house as welcome guests, and whom to stop at the door. You can choose who can stay for a cup of tea, who can share your quarters for an extended time, and who has to be evicted for bad behavior. Good, strong boundaries of the mind protect your health, emotions, sense of self, money, and relationships.

You know where your house ends and where the outside world begins, don't you? If you didn't, any squatter could lounge inside your house without your awareness. You wouldn't know if you should show them the door, because you wouldn't even know where the door was. This kind of living would be a disaster. Fortunately, the boundaries of your house are well defined. Your doors lock securely, and your windows can close to prevent unauthorized access to your home. Maybe you even have a fence, or live in a gated community. Do you have the same clarity when it comes to the boundaries of your mind?

Here are a few reasons people might struggle with maintaining good boundaries:

1. They are empaths who never learned how to protect their inner space. As a result, they are both a walking sponge for other people's energy, and a free charging station. If they don't learn how to establish better boundaries, they might feel overwhelmed or depleted after merely talking to people.

2. They are codependent people. Co-dependence is a pattern usually developed in childhood, when people feel compelled to manage other people's lives, and let others manage their own life.

3. They have the need to be in control. Closely related to codependency, the need to control is a compulsory urge to manage other people's mental properties such as behaviors, beliefs, emotions, and life choices.

4. They need other people's approval. The need for approval creates a hole in the energy boundaries through which other people can insert a hook of manipulation.

5. They grew up in an environment where their boundaries were never honored and were often ignored, so they never learned to protect their mental property.

6. Their boundaries were forcibly broken through a traumatic experience, and need to be repaired.

Hypnosis helps teach the mind to create and maintain strong boundaries from a place of kindness, compassion, and mutual respect.

Boundary-building Process#1 (by Shelley Stockwell-Nicholas, Ph.D.)

DO THIS:

1. Close your eyes, and take a few deep breaths. Relax your body, and turn your attention inward.

2. Think of everything which is you. Your thoughts, your ideas, your emotions, your memories, your energy, etc. Where do you end?

3. Many people struggle to find their boundaries. They feel as if they go on and on. If this is the case with you, imagine another human being talking to you. Where do you end, and they begin?

4. Next, surround yourself with an imaginary bubble. It can be transparent, or have any color of your choice.

5. Pull all your energy, your thoughts, your sense of self, your memories, your lessons, your mistakes, and everything that is you inside this bubble.

6. Do the same for your imaginary human being, placing everything constituting them into their own bubble.

7. If you want, you can send a rainbow bridge connecting the two of you from heart to heart. You can withdraw this connection at any time. You can put a gate or a guard on it. You can decide that only wholesome and nourishing energy will be allowed to cross this bridge.

8. Enjoy the feeling of being separate and independent from the other human being, while still enjoying your human connection.

It is not enough to have great boundaries; it is also very important to have some process of checking your energy, and clearing it promptly from external influences. This is especially important for empaths. Being a sponge for other people's emotional energy means that this sponge might get clogged, and needs to be rinsed regularly.

Imagine you invited a friend to your house, and this friend brought their luggage with them, and spread their belongings all over your home. Are you going to keep it this way when they leave? Or would you make sure they didn't leave their hairbrush in your bathroom, and their underwear in your guest bedroom?

Imagine this friend also had a troubled relationship, and spent their time in your house sharing all the emotional details of their romantic disaster. After they leave, you still feel emotionally shaken. You keep thinking about your friend, and feeling sorry for them. How long do you intend to keep feeling your friend's emotions?

It is great to empathize and be attentive to other people's pain. But it might be very taxing on you if you never clear this energy out of your mind; if you let it fester there, stealing your own happiness and peace. We know now that every time we feel an emotion, our body goes to the trouble and expense of producing the chemicals associated with this emotion. These chemicals influence our internal organs, immune system, thinking, sleep, eating, and relating. Imagine your body as a big sponge soaked in various biologically active drugs. Some of these drugs are coming from your own emotional responses to your own life experiences. Others are coming from other people's stories, or from your reaction to their emotions. If you are absorbing too much, you might soon find yourself drained, depressed, confused, or emotionally burned out.

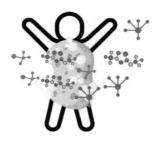

DO THIS:

1. Take a deep breath, and let it out slowly. Relax your body. Wrap yourself in your boundary bubble described in Process #1.

2. Imagine you have a tiny drone that can fly to other people, and take a sample probe of their emotions. You don't have to saturate your entire body with another person's emotion. It's enough to have a small portion of it so you can empathize with them without going all the way down into the same rabbit hole.

3. After you've received the sample of their emotion, notice your own response. If you feel depleted or drained, you need to take a smaller probe.

4. Practice this visualization every time you talk to people who are experiencing a strong emotion, or sharing a passionate story. With practice, you will be able to feel for them but not become them. You'll be able to retain your ability to think resourcefully, and be in a

supportive state without holding their pain within your own body for too long.

One great reason to have good boundaries is to be more protected from critical comments, especially if you have to regularly communicate with negative and highly critical people (or if you are married to them). Imagine what it would be like to hear the same critical comments without feeling bad?

DO THIS:

Create the same boundary bubble as in the first two exercises.

1. Think of a time when you were driving a car (or were a passenger in a car) and bugs were hitting the windshield. Remember how the windshield wipers simply swept the squashed bugs away?

2. Imagine critical comments as bugs hitting your windshield. Before the windshield wiper sweeps by, you have just enough time to briefly examine the comment, and extract any useful information. You can leave all the negativity on the windshield to be washed away.

3. Keep driving through the conversation, wiping away all the bugs, and retaining only useful and helpful information. Notice how good it feels.

Your mind is a house you carry with you. It makes sense to keep this house clean and comfortable. The more you learn to maintain clear boundaries between your mind and other minds while allowing connection, interaction, and emotional awareness of another person, the more confident, peaceful, and balanced you will feel. Great boundaries are built on self-respect, self-love, and self-awareness. These qualities help you become happier. They allow you to have more positive social situations, better relationships, and a much healthier body.

A Meditation Corner:
Feel Like a Million Bucks

1. Take a nice easy breath, and relax. Close your eyes. Imagine a $1 million dollar bill right in front of you. See it, feel it, or imagine it in your own unique way. Make it big. Smile into this $1 million dollar bill.

2. Reflect on all the material goods, services, and experiences you can purchase with this $1 million dollar bill. Imagine them in a most pleasing way. Smile into all this goodness.

3. On the count of three, use your mind to quickly condense the $1 million dollar bill and everything it can buy into a small ball of light. Next, take a deep breath, inhale the small ball of light, and beam it into your brain. Release the million-dollar value into your brain. Feel good in your brain. Smile into your brain.

4. Imagine this $1 million dollar bill in front of you again. Bring your attention to it, and smile into it again. Reflect more on all the goodness into which it can be converted.

5. Once again, imagine condensing the $1 million dollar bill and all the goodness it can bring into a small ball of light. Take a deep breath, inhale the ball of light, and beam

it into your heart. Release the million-dollar value into your heart. Feel good in your heart. Smile into your heart.

6. Repeat the above process to bring this $1 million dollar energy into your gut. Repeat it with any part of your body that wants to feel like a million bucks.

7. Relax, and smile all over yourself. Feel like a million bucks.

8. Imagine yourself moving into your future feeling like a million bucks.

9. Imagine smiling this $1 million dollar energy into other people so they can also feel like a million bucks in your presence.

CHAPTER 8

How to Let Go, and Be Joyful and Free

As a hypnotherapist, I often encounter people whose minds are haunted by the ghosts of their past relationships. Unhealed wounds from childhood, memories of heartbreaks and betrayals, injustice, cruelty, or hurt inflicted by others keep troubling their minds long after the painful experience is over.

Logically, it makes no sense. Wouldn't it be better to just leave whatever was painful and unpleasant in the past where it belongs? Wouldn't it be more enjoyable to be light-hearted, free, and unburdened by old stories and hurts? Of course it would. But if you've ever had to deal with a recurring memory that just wouldn't go away, stealing your peace and intruding on your current relationships, you know that letting go is not always easy. In this chapter, you will learn simple mental processes for forgiving, and letting go.

First, it is important to let go of any reasons to hold on. One of the most powerful words in the human language is "because." In one experiment, conducted by social psychologist Ellen Langer, people were able to cut in line to use a Xerox machine just by using the word "because."

When told "Excuse me, I have five pages; may I use the Xerox machine because I'm in a rush?" a full 94% of the people in line allowed the person to cut in.

This was understandable; people are kind.

But 93% responded just as kindly when asked, "May I use the Xerox machine because I have to make some copies?"

This makes no sense! Everyone was in line to make copies. However, the mind is hard-wired to respond to the word "because."

To prove this, the word "because" was removed from the same sentence: "Excuse me, I have five pages; may I use the Xerox machine?" This time, only 60% of the people agreed to let someone cut in front of them.

When you believe you need to hold onto a past grudge — or

continue an old argument in your head — you use the magic of "because" to solidify the bond keeping you a prisoner of your past.

DO THIS:

To break the spell, select a recurring memory or old argument that keeps running through your head. Ask yourself, "What is so important to me that I think about this now, in my present?"

Write down all the reasons.

You might come up with a number of "because" reasons.

Because it is unfair.

Because I feel betrayed.

Because they never apologized.

Because I was mistreated.

And so on.

Put all the verbs in the past tense, and remove the word "because."

It was unfair.

I was betrayed.

They never apologized.

I was mistreated.

By removing "because" and leaving just the bare facts, you begin to dissolve the chains keeping you attached to the past.

Now take a few deep breaths, and imagine draining all the emotion out of every line, like draining dirty water from a bathtub. Read every line with a perfectly neutral and matter-of-fact intonation. How does it feel now?

One problem with the human mind is that it is a time traveler. There is a very thin slice of time called the present moment where your mind, your energy, and your heartbeat intersect, and happen at the same time in the same place. In addition to that, your mind is always extended into the future. It keeps running into your past like a worried traveler who keeps wondering if they turned off the stove or locked the front door.

This is quite normal — and important. The past is a source of knowledge, resources, and valuable lessons. People who lose their ability to remember due to brain damage are marooned on the island of the now; they cannot remember whether they had breakfast, or with whom they just had a conversation. If your mind wasn't able to imagine your future, you wouldn't be able to plan your vacations, or even Saturday movie nights. Living only in the present moment might sound good, but it isn't very practical. But at the same time, since you have a finite capacity to hold a number of thoughts simultaneously in your head, constantly revisiting something unpleasant robs you from experiencing other thoughts, memories, or dreams about your future. There simply isn't that much space in your head available for your conscious awareness at any given moment. It makes sense to use it in a way that creates more joy, pleasure, and fun in the present moment — and that moves you to a better future.

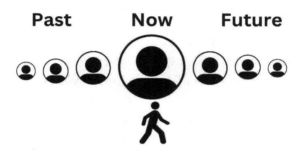

Remembering the same bad memory is like repeatedly watching the same scary or disturbing movie, ignoring a whole box of other movies available to you. Let's learn how to choose your mental movies. It is helpful to have someone guiding you through these steps, but you can record your own instructions and play them back with your eyes closed. Be sure to leave some pauses for creating imaginary scenery.

DO THIS:

1. Take a few deep breaths, and relax. Close your eyes.

2. Imagine watching a movie on a movie screen. Pick one disturbing and recurring memory to watch.

3. How old is this movie? How many years ago did it happen? Notice the time period and age of the movie.

What do you need to change to communicate to your unconscious mind that this is not a current report, but an old movie?

4. Next, distance yourself from the imaginary screen. Imagine watching it from the last row of a movie house, or from the projectionist's booth.

5. Ask yourself, "If I had to go through this again, what would I need to know or be able to do in order to minimize the impact?" Search through your memories for the resources, wisdom, and skills that were not available to you in the past. Add them to your viewing experience, and notice the difference they make. It is often important to remind your younger self that you survived the experience, and it was not the end of your world.

6. Make a moral judgment from your current mature self. If this happened not to you, but to another person, how would you evaluate it? If the memory involves your parents, relatives, or past lovers, imagine them as strangers. What is your core belief about this action or experience now?

People are often asked to forgive something which goes against their moral core. Even though intellectually they might agree to forgive, deep inside they might still hold pain and resentment. Making a clear moral judgment helps release deeply seated feelings of injustice.

DO THIS:

1. Take a long honest look at your own actions and behaviors. Is there any situation in which you commit the same injustice or cruelty, or show the same insensitivity? Are you willing to commit to upholding your own moral standards without excuses or self-deceit? Put your hand on your heart, and make a promise to your past, present, and future self. Take a deep breath.

2. Now you are ready to let go. Take a deep breath, and let the whole experience move further and further away. Imagine cutting any energy cords which still might hold you attached to the memory. Exhale the energy of this experience from your body, and send it to the light. You are done with it! You are free!

As you might know, nature abhors a vacuum. This is why you need to fill your newly free mental space with some other activity. In the past, your mind would travel to the past to bring back your bad experience, with all its associated emotions and physical sensations. What would you like it to do instead? Are there good memories you would like to revisit more often? Is there a creative process in which you'd like to engage instead? Is there a useful habit you would like to cultivate using the same mental space? Imagine moving into your future while doing this new activity with your mind. If you continue doing it every day for the next two weeks, what would be different? If you keep doing it for the next two months, what would be different? And if you keep doing it for an entire year, what would be different? Do you like the outcome? Then you can keep it. If not, pick some other mental activity, and repeat the future pacing process.

Taoist Simple Release Process

In the Taoist Inner Energy Alchemy practices, releasing negative memories and emotions is a daily practice. Ancient Tao Masters believed that your inner space needs to be kept clean and free of disturbing energies from the past, which might drain energy, and intrude on your present peace. Some of their "letting go" meditations are quite complex and elaborate, but there is a very simple one which anybody can do.

DO THIS:

1. Sit quite straight in a chair with your feet planted into the earth. Imagine your feet growing deep roots into the earth.

2. Take a few deep breaths, and relax your body. Close your eyes.

3. Start gently rocking your spine, imagining it loosening and relaxing. Smile into your spine, and feel your spine getting warm and loose.

4. Turn your attention inward, and begin to mentally go through your day. Was there anything which upset, irritated, saddened, angered, or frustrated you? Is there

any hurt or disturbance still stuck in your energy field? Is there anything toxic, cloudy, foggy, too cold, too hot, too heavy, etc.? Notice it in your body, not just your head.

5. As you continue gently rocking your spine, begin exhaling all these energies and sensations out of your body into the earth. Imagine them moving through your spine, through your legs, and through the bottoms of your feet, all the way into the ground.

6. After this is completed, make a cross with your hand and your mind over this imaginary place in the earth into which you've released your negative emotions. Say in a commanding yet kind tonality, "You will never come back. Let the earth compost you."

7. Then imagine all that energy composting in the earth, and becoming beautiful flowers.

8. Sit quietly, and breathe golden light through the bottoms of your feet. Let the light travel up your spine, and into all the organs and places previously harboring the bad feelings. Notice how good it feels.

There is nothing as freeing and enjoyable as letting go of the ghosts from the past. Your body feels light, your heart is at ease, and your mind is delightfully calm. In time, you will notice that you have more space for creativity, joy, laughter, and loving connections in the present. You might start noticing the warmth of the sun on your skin, the breeze on your face, and the colors and sounds around you. You will start feeling more alive, with a sense of child-like wonder returning.

CHAPTER 9

How to Have Great Skin, and Love Your Reflection In the Mirror

Do you love your reflection in the mirror? We are so conditioned to admire youth and beauty that loving our own reflection in the mirror — especially if it is not radiantly young or gloriously beautiful — might present a challenge. In this chapter you will learn how to take good care of your skin, and love seeing yourself in the mirror. If you already have great skin (and adore yourself in the mirror), you can pick up a few new tools to help yourself shine even brighter.

Endorphin Skin Treatment

Even though youth and beauty are natural gifts which enchant and attract on a very deep level, there are many versions of this mesmerizing quality. The most important characteristic of a young person is not their age, but their radiance and liveliness. Research shows that a young child smiles 400 times a day, while even the happiest adult smiles only 40 times a day. Most adults smile less than 20 times a day. Many adults go for days without a genuine smile or a hearty laugh. When was the last time you guffawed, chortled, rolled on the floor laughing, or laughed out loud? When we genuinely smile, laugh, and feel joy, our cells release neurochemical endorphins. This is why happiness is so important for our skin and beauty. A beta-endorphin looks like this:

Beta Endorphin. This image is in the public domain.

Endorphins relax the tiny blood capillaries which feed our skin. As a result, the skin receives more oxygen, more hydration, and more nutrition, and regains its wonderful youthful vigor, radiance, and glow. In order to help your body release these endorphins, your smiles and laughter must be genuine. The good news is that you can help your neurology create genuine smiles and laughter.

Make Your Skin Smile!

DO THIS:

1. Take a deep breath, and exhale slowly.

2. Imagine a waterfall of warm, relaxing energy flowing from the top of your head all the way down to your toes. Take another deep breath, and close your eyes. Relax with every easy breath.

3. Let your mind drift to a memory of laughing with someone you adore. Step into this memory, and be there 100%.

4. Inhale the energy of this laughter. Exhale the energy of this laughter into your skin. Repeat this nine times.

5. Think of the last time you really enjoyed being with another human being. What were you doing? What were you talking about? What made it so enjoyable?

6. Inhale the energy of this enjoyment, and exhale it into your skin. Repeat this nine times.

7. Think of a time when you received a great hug or a wonderful kiss. Allow yourself to step into this memory, and activate all your senses. Pretend this memory is happening right now.

8. Inhale the energy of this hug or kiss, and exhale it into your skin. Repeat this nine times.

9. Finish this meditation by smiling all over yourself, from your head to your toes — and from your toes to your head.

Relaxation Skin Treatment

In order to function well and look terrific, your skin needs to have intervals of deep rest and relaxation. This doesn't mean you have to sit in a mountain cave avoiding all stress. Our body is well designed to deal with stress and challenges. But it is not designed to stay tense and stressed all the time. The organ which is most deeply affected by stress is the skin. Stress makes the tiny skin capillaries constrict, and block the flow of oxygen, hydration, and nutrition to the skin. Chronic stress might cause a chronic inflammatory condition which many researchers now call "inflammaging," because it really ages our skin. In addition, lasting tension and stress slow down skin regeneration. Finally, chronic muscular tension under our facial skin coupled with decreased elasticity as we age might create a "mask" of frozen emotion. Your most prevailing emotion becomes ingrained into your skin structure. It's possible for these "expression wrinkles" or "frown lines" to be smoothed out by injections of botulinum toxin. But these injections paralyze the entire set of muscles in the facial area, making emotional expressions limited, or even impossible. One of the most attractive qualities of a young person is their lively and expressive face, with its fluidity and spontaneity of emotions. Making a face smooth but immovable does not promote beauty and youthfulness. There is another way! The way of relaxation.

Deep Relaxation Journey.

DO THIS:

1. Lie down comfortably, and make sure you will not be disturbed. Take a few deep breaths, and close your eyes.

2. Imagine scanning your body with your mind, noticing which parts are more relaxed, and which parts might be holding tension. Smile into your body.

3. Imagine that your breath, attention, and smile are rays of sunshine. Not too hot nor too intense; just warm, nurturing, and gentle.

4. Bring your breath and smiling attention to every area where you detect tension, and imagine this tension melting like ice cream on a hot summer day.

5. Now imagine a gentle breeze, like the breath of the universe moving through you. Imagine allowing it to go through you carrying away all your tension, and all your dark, cloudy, and foggy energy.

6. Practice this visualization for a few minutes every day, until your body begins to feel open, soft, relaxed, and filled with sunshine.

7. When you achieve this stage, imagine shining this sunshine through you skin, relaxing it deeply and completely.

You will notice a greater glow and more youthfulness after you practice this visualization and breathing for the first time. With regular use, your skin will begin to look noticeably younger, and much more radiant.

Regeneration Skin Treatment

Your skin is an organ that lives on the edge. Just like your mind, your skin is both internal and external. It is immersed within your inner body environment, and receives nutrition from it. It is also exposed to the outside world, and touches the world with its senses. This means that (first) your skin is visible to other people, and (next) it can be damaged by external factors. Fortunately, our skin resists wear and tear very well because it is capable of regeneration. Therefore, whatever supports skin regeneration will help it look younger and more beautiful. Consequently, anything that impedes or blocks skin regeneration will accelerate its aging, and diminish its beauty and radiance. Skin is regenerated through:

1. Rest and relaxation.

2. Positive emotions such as love, joy, and happiness.

3. Regular exfoliation. This is a skin care treatment which gently peels away the upper skin layers, and activates underlying renewal. It is better to use gentle and slow-acting products such as natural scrubs, enzyme-based peels, and low concentration (10-20%) alpha hydroxy acid (AHA) peels rather than more intense treatments which cause visible skin peeling and redness.

4. Hydration.

5. Movement which activates circulation.

6. Wholesome nutrition.

7. Visualization which communicates the message of renewal to the skin.

Blue Dot Healing Meditation

DO THIS:

1. Take a deep breath. Hold it for a moment, look up, and smile into your brain. Exhale, look down, close your eyes, and relax your eyelids. Pretend that your eyelids are so relaxed they don't want to open. Relax your eyes.

2. Smile into your eyes. Smile into your brain. Let your smile be like a waterfall going from the top of your head all the way down to your toes, saturating your skin with loving and smiling sunshine energy.

3. Imagine a blue bubble all around you. Feel safe.

4. Inhale the blue color. Exhale and release all your tension, and all your stress.

5. Imagine shrinking down with every breath, becoming smaller and smaller until you become as small as a drop of water. Next, shrink even further into a small blue dot of light.

6. Imagine this little blue dot entering your body with your breath, and being absorbed into your bloodstream.

7. Next, imagine being fully absorbed into your tissues. Imagine traveling through yourself; through your tissues to the very core of your being, until you discover a source of healing energy within you. Healing is what you do. Even plants know how to heal. All animals,

including humans, know how to heal. When you scraped your knee as a child, it knew how to heal. When you cut your skin, it knew how to heal. When you were sneezing and feeling under the weather, your body knew how to heal.

8. Be a little blue dot suspended in your core, bathed in your healing light. Allow yourself to experience your own healing. Different people experience it differently. Some people experience it as vibration. Others see light, and others feel senses beyond senses. Notice how you experience your own healing energy. Your experience will be perfect for you.

9. Now imagine condensing this energy within you, knowing that even though your healing energy is big, it can also be condensed to a tiny blue dot.

10. Imagine traveling as a blue dot to any area of your body which is experiencing discomfort. Then imagine, on the count of three, a charge of healing energy released into any area which needs healing. 1, 2, 3 - saturation! You've just saturated this area with your healing energy.

11. Repeat absorbing, condensing, delivering, and releasing your healing energy wherever it is needed. Once your body has memorized the healing process, it will be simple and effortless.

12. Allow the blue dot to grow bigger until it fills your entire body. Imagine fully inhabiting your own body.

When you're ready, count to three, take a nice easy full breath, exhale, and smile all over yourself. Open your eyes, and come all the way back, feeling wonderful.

Love Skin Treatment

Many people think that if they start looking younger and lose a few pounds, they will love themselves more. But love is not given on the condition of improvement. Love is the energy that makes everything it touches beautiful. Love is a secret sauce that improves all conditions. It makes sense to start cultivating self-love immediately. Then remember to apply it to your skin daily.

Smile Love Into Yourself

DO THIS:

1. Think of a person or an animal you love. Close your eyes, and imagine them in front of you. Smile as you would if they were really there.

2. Inhale love energy into your brain, and exhale it into your eyes. Smile into your eyes.

3. Inhale love energy into your brain, and exhale it into your heart. Smile into your heart.

4. Put your palms over your heart, and keep smiling love into your heart. Wait until your heart starts smiling at you.

5. Inhale love from your heart, and exhale it into your gut. Smile into your gut.

6. Put your palms over your gut, and keep smiling love into your gut until your gut starts smiling at you.

7. Inhale love from your gut, and exhale it into your skin. Smile into your skin. Give yourself a hug. Caress your skin lovingly, and keep smiling love into your whole being.

8. When you are ready, take a deep breath, and smile all over yourself.

9. Look into the mirror, and smile all over your reflection in the mirror.

This process works directly with your neurology, bypassing psychology. Commit to doing it daily, and you will notice your reflection in the mirror becoming more and more adorable. Soon, you will smile at yourself from the fullness of your loving heart. Then it will be much easier to share this loving light with others.

CHAPTER 10

How to Live Your Soul Purpose

Do you know your soul purpose? Many people struggle with this question. One reason this happens is that most people learn to believe their purpose has to be something impressive and grand. In fact, anything that gives you a sense of purpose and direction is a good purpose. So the first step in living your purpose happily is letting go of the idea that your purpose has to impress other people. The sole purpose of your purpose is your own happiness in having it. In this chapter you will learn how to discover the main thing that makes you happy, and gives you a feeling of fulfillment every day.

What is so important to you that you would go out of your

way to have it? What makes you feel good? What lights your fire? What makes your life worth living?

Maybe it's having time with your family. Maybe it's watching your children grow into good people. Maybe it's doing acts of kindness. Maybe it's creative freedom. Maybe it's the smell of fresh coffee in the morning. Or maybe it's being surrounded by beauty.

Write down three things which top your list of the most important things in your life. Be as specific as you can.

Start with the top item on your list. Get a fresh piece of paper, or open a new document on your computer. Ask, "Why is having this so important to me?" Write down your answer.

Then look at your answer, take a deep breath, and ask the same question again: "Why is having this so important to me?" Write down your answer.

Repeat this step until you start getting recurring or circular answers. Then look at what keeps coming up, and write it down.

It could be something like freedom, or love, or connection, or peace.

Repeat the same process with the next two activities or experiences.

It might look like this:

It is really important for me to spend time with my family.

"Why is having this so important to me?"

It makes me feel loved.

"Why is having this so important to me?"

I feel I am not alone.

"Why is having this so important to me?"

I feel that my life matters somehow.

"Why is having this so important to me?"

I need to know I am making a difference.

"Why is having this so important to me?"

To not waste my life. To make something with it.

"Why is having this so important to me?"

To be remembered.

"Why is having this so important to me?"

I don't want to just vanish so nobody remembers who I was. I want to make some positive difference for my kids, my friends, my partner…

If these were your answers, as a summary statement you could write down: "It is important for me to have significance, be remembered, and make some positive difference in the lives of my kids, my friends, and my family."

DO THIS:

Notice the feelings being evoked as you look at your summary statement. Notice where in your body you feel this feeling. If you assigned a color to this feeling, what color would it be? If you assigned a texture to this feeling, what texture would it be? How does this feeling move within your body?

Imagine creating more space for this feeling. Allow it to spread to other areas of your body, or to flow through it like a river. Imagine with every breath you take you dive deeper into this feeling, making it grow bigger and stronger. If this feeling were a radio signal, how can you make it clearer?

Imagine bringing this feeling into every moment, with every fiber of your being, while performing an activity that bears great significance for you. What do you notice when you do it? You now know what is truly important to you. What do you need to do differently?

Imagine making any necessary adjustments, and moving into the future with a feeling of confidence about what you are doing, and feeling fully committed to doing it. What happens after a year of doing this? What happens after five years? What happens after 10 years of living like this? If you live like this your entire life, what difference will it make for you — and the people you love?

Now look at your end result. Do you like your purpose? Does it make you feel fulfilled? Does it inspire a satisfied sigh at the end of the day? If yes, congratulations! You have a purpose, and can live it happily. If you've realized this is not what you want, that's OK too. Using the same process, try other important and satisfying activities and experiences until you find something which offers you a feeling of fulfillment.

It is helpful to create your personal mantra to remind you of your purpose. Simpler mantras are more powerful than long and complex ones. Using the above example, your mantra could be as simple as: "I am making a positive difference every day."

When you are driven by the need for approval, you might get approval — but you might not receive any fun, pleasure, or satisfaction. When you are driven by the need for fun, pleasure, and satisfaction, you might get fun, pleasure, and satisfaction — but you might not receive anyone's approval. **When you are driven by your soul purpose, you might receive fun, pleasure, satisfaction, and approval with grace — but you will not require them to achieve your own happiness, or depend on them for your joy.**

Living with a sense of purpose makes people happier. No matter how big or how small a purpose might be, it allows people to organize their time. This creates more space for the most important activities, and eliminates time wasters. It gives people a sense of direction, and helps them focus their energy on what brings them the most satisfying results. It also helps to release any guilt resulting from not living up to other people's demands and expectations.

With time, your purpose might change, and that is OK too. You are supposed to grow and evolve. It is helpful to do this exercise once a year to ensure that you are still living your purpose happily.

Like a Tree

(Inspired by Dr. Shelley Stockwell-Nicholas'
"The Tree of You" process.)

1. Sit straight or recline comfortably. Rest on your bed, or perhaps relax in a hot bath enhanced with your favorite bath salts or oils.

2. Take a deep breath, and close your eyes. Exhale slowly, and allow your body to relax.

3. Think of a tree. Allow this tree to come to your mind in any comfortable and pleasing way. Notice that the tree has a component visible above the ground, and a component hidden underground. There are roots, and there is a trunk supporting the branches and leaves. There might even be flowers and fruit.

4. Imagine walking toward this tree, and noticing a door. Open the door, and walk inside the tree. Allow yourself to become the tree.

5. Take another nice and easy breath, and bring your awareness to your feet. Imagine standing tall like a tree, and allow your roots to go deep into the earth. What feeds you? What anchors you? How healthy are your roots? If they are not healthy, imagine sending light to them, and making them healthy and whole. How do you stay grounded? If you need more grounding, make your roots stronger and deeper. Allow yourself to reflect on all the experiences that brought you to this moment. Then expand your awareness into your lineage. Think of all your ancestors who created the path on which you are now walking. Take as much time as you need.

6. Take another deep breath, open your eyes, and then close your eyes. Bring your attention to your core. Who are you at your core? What is your unique energy and essence? Before you had any conditioning — before you accepted other people's ideas about you — who were you at your core? Allow yourself to remember your truth. Notice how your core is supported by your roots. Take all the time you need.

7. Around your core is your next layer: your values. You learn to value certain things based on your experiences, and on the conditioning received from your parents, teachers, friends, and society. What did you learn to

value about yourself and others? What did you learn to value in life? Ask yourself, "Are my values fully aligned with my core? Are there any values which need to be re-evaluated?" For example, I learned to value education and academic knowledge. My parents were scientists, and they were very dismissive of people who did not go to college, and who did not have academic knowledge. But as an adult, I have met many people who never went to college. They are very intelligent and beautiful people. So today, I value not just academic knowledge, but also the type of knowledge achieved through reflection, meditation, and life experience. I have adjusted my values.

8. After your values, the next layer around your core consists of your beliefs. Just like values, beliefs come from programming you received as a child. Many beliefs are useful; some beliefs can be damaging or limiting. Ask yourself, "Is what I believe fully aligned with my core and my values?"

9. Your next layer consists of your actions. They are what you show to the world. Are your actions aligned with your core truths, your values, and your beliefs? Do you have integrity?

10. Now think about your branches and your leaves. A tree uses its leaves to receive sunlight, CO_2, and oxygen. During the day, those leaves generate oxygen for all of life to breathe in. Its branches give shade, and those branches might even have flowers and fruit. How do

you give and receive? Is it balanced? Do you allow yourself to be nourished and replenished?

11. Finally, think about your bark. This is your mask, or the personality you show to the world. This is how you show up socially with your family and friends, how you act professionally, and how you present on social media. Is your bark fully aligned with your core?

12. Imagine yourself becoming fully aligned and integrated. Stand tall, and claim your space. Reach deep into the earth. Reach high into the sky. Imagine being connected and supported by other trees, the earth, the sky, and the sun. Be a part of everything. Feel the life force flowing through you.

13. When you are ready, take a deep breath, and come back to the room with awareness.

14. Stand up, shake your hands and your body, stretch, and take another deep breath.

Conclusion
Happiness Is Not a Place

Many people believe that once they achieve a goal or fulfill their heart's desire, they will be happy forever.

But happiness is not a place. You cannot live there.

Yes, you can BE happy. But unless you die while being happy, your mood and emotion will change. Inevitably, any happy moment becomes a memory, and begins to drift into the past, becoming more and more distant.

It's easy to start wondering:

"Do I need a better job?"

"Do I need a better lover?"

"Do I need to better myself?"

Yes, you can set more goals and yes, you can be relentless in striving to reach these goals. But no matter how many goals you achieve, happiness will always be fleeting. You can be happy, but you cannot be happy forever. You cannot glue that happy place on your face, and freeze your inner state in the "happy" mode.

When you believe that you can only be happy once you find your dream job, an ideal partner, or the perfect diet, happiness becomes a fantasy. You can chase it over the course of years and years, forever — never quite reaching it, and always wanting it.

Paradoxically, the happiest people do not make happiness their end goal. The happiest people make happiness just one of the colors in the masterpiece of their lives.

Happiness

The secret to lasting happiness is to simply be happy when something wonderful happens, and sad when something makes you sad. Then you can be angry when something angers you, and indifferent when you don't care. Then something else might make you smile, and take you back to being happy. It helps to learn how to make happy moments more plentiful by adopting simple practices of making yourself happier, and learning to do everyday tasks with a happy attitude.

The hypnotic processes presented in this book have helped hundreds of my clients become happier in their everyday lives. They've learned to make sure they always have enough energy, nurture their creativity, and have more fun daily. They've learned to sleep better, eat healthier (while enjoying it), make better and more achievable goals, have better boundaries, and take great care of their skin so they radiate their light everywhere they go. Most importantly, they've learned to live with a sense of purpose. With this knowledge, they've discovered it was easy to be happy. They've also realized that everything they ever wanted to achieve was much easier to achieve when they were happy.

When you learn to savor happiness when life serves it, and swallow bitter medicine when you have to, you can focus your energy where it is most needed, making small and essential steps in the present to ensure better and more delightful life experiences in the future.

If you need professional support in your quest for being happy, you can reach me at anna@amargolina.com, or set up your free consultation at www.annamargolina.com

With love,
Dr. Anna

About Dr. Anna Margolina, Ph.D.

Dr. Anna Margolina, Ph.D., is a hypnotherapist, speaker, author, Master NLP Practitioner, and Qigong instructor.

She grew up in Russia in a family of scientists. She started her career as a scientist in Russia. She has a Master's Degree in Medical Biophysics, and a Ph.D. in biology from the Russian State Medical University. She worked as a science editor and researcher for the Russian Cosmetics and Medicine Journal, and acquired a deep knowledge and understanding of skin and its beauty needs.

When she came to America in 2001, she became interested in hypnosis. She went to Thailand to study the spiritual practices of the ancient Tao Masters.

Today, Dr. Anna is a trusted authority on hypnosis and personal transformation. She works with clients from all around the world, and leads workshops and seminars, sharing her extensive knowledge and experience. She lives in Washington state near Seattle, and enjoys her deep connections with the beautiful nature of the Pacific Northwest.

Website: www.AnnaMargolina.com

Email: Anna@AMargolina.com